Invisible Combatants, the World of the Child Soldier

A Selective Annotated Bibliography of Dissertations and Theses

Milo Avicenna

Milo, Avicenna

Invisible Combatants, the World of the Child Soldier: A selective annotated bibliography of dissertations and theses/Milo Avicenna

p. cm.

1. Child Soldiers. 2. Children at War. I. Title.

K 639

341.1

ISBN-10   1507611889

ISBN-13   978-1507611883

1.)   **Ackley, M. J.**

Post-conflict reintegration and gender: Why male child soldiers have been denied sexual and reproductive health assistance in post-conflict societies?

M.A. thesis, Webster University. 2009.

In analyzing five of the most recent civil conflicts in Africa, civilians are in great danger. The targeting of civilians, specifically women and children, has increased dramatically for various reasons. This has led to a rapid expansion of conflict and post-conflict research in two fields: child soldiers and gender. The research on the issue of child soldiers has expanded as quickly as the number of children recruited every year. The same is true with respect to the field of gender. Presently, experts incorporate a gender-based approach to address the causes of and solutions to problems created by armed conflict. As the definition of gender has evolved, it has expanded to the political, economic, and social realms of societies. An engendered approach to post-conflict reconstruction has worked to ensure the inclusion of women and girls and recently men. Still, when discussing an engendered approach to post-conflict health, specifically sexual and reproductive health, the definition of gender has forgotten boys. Post-conflict programs should be expanded to make policy and theory into reality and action. [Author Abstract]

2.)   **Annan, J.**

Self-appraisal, social support, and connectedness as protective factors for youth associated with fighting forces in northern Uganda.

Ph.D. dissertation, Indiana University. 2007.

Over the past few decades, there has been a proliferation in the use of child soldiers and it is estimated that they make up 10% of fighting forces in more than 20 countries. Northern Uganda has been one of the most tragic cases of the use of young soldiers with tens of thousands of youth abducted by the Lord's Resistance Army over the past decade. This study provides a basis for understanding these youth and their return home by examining the impact of rebel abduction and exposure to traumatic events on youth's psychosocial adjustment on a representative sample of youth in northern Uganda. It also examined self-appraisal, social support, family connectedness, and community involvement as protective factors for the youth's psychosocial adjustment. [Author Abstract]

3.) **Appah, A. S.**

An assessment of services for child soldiers.
M.P.H. thesis, University of North Texas Health Science Center at Fort Worth. 2009.

Humanitarian relief organizations (HRO) have an important role in providing services during complex humanitarian emergencies (CHE), especially to children in armed conflict. This study examines the strengths and limitations of HROs ability to provide services for child soldiers globally by surveying and interviewing various local and international HROs. HROs were found to provide more indirect services than direct services and limited number gender specific services for female child soldiers. Also, HROs reported barriers to collaboration between organizations due lack of sharing resources, limited exchange of "best practices" and competition of financial resources. Further research is needed to determine how HROs can improve planning and implementation of services to child soldiers, especially females, and effectively collaborate with other HROs to provide comprehensive services. [Author Abstract]

4.)   Atukoit-Malinga, C. G.

Child soldiers and child conscription into armed conflicts in Africa.

M.S.W. thesis, McGill University (Canada). 1999.

Research studies that have already been conducted on the problem of child soldiers and child conscription have focused mostly on psychological trauma. Less attention has been paid to social, economic, and political processes in Africa. The goal of this thesis is to explore perceptions of professionals from various disciplines working in different organizations and government institutions (N = 207) concerning the causes, effects, and solutions to child conscription in Africa. These professionals perceived that poverty, lack of educational resources, lack of community resources, economic hardships, dictates of international funders, corrupt governments, and unemployment were the major causes of child conscription into armed conflicts. With respect to the effects, the respondents perceived that physical and psychological issues, witnessing atrocities, and exposure to violence were the most important effects of participating in the armed conflicts. In order to prevent or stop further recruitment of children into armed conflicts, the professionals working in the field thought that more educational programs should be initiated, community resources should be mobilized, prevention programs should be established, employment and training opportunities programs should also be provided, strong international laws drafted, advocacy and empowerment promoted, support for families provided, and awareness campaigns facilitated. A striking result of this study is that professionals perceived counselling as a relatively unimportant solution to the problem of child conscription. Results are discussed in terms of the contrast between past research in the field, which has focused on individual-level effects and counselling solutions, and the societal-level effects, and solutions that professionals perceive are central to the problem. [Author Abstract]

5.)   **Bainomugisha, A.**

Child soldiers in northern Uganda: an analysis of the challenges and opportunities for reintegration and rehabilitation.

Ph.D. dissertation, University of Bradford (United Kingdom). 2010.

The level of brutality and violence against children abducted and forcefully conscripted by the Lord's Resistance Army (LRA) in northern Uganda pricked the conscience of humanity. The suffering of the people in northern Uganda was described by Jan Egeland, the former United Nations Under-Secretary for Humanitarian Affairs, as "the biggest forgotten humanitarian crisis in the world." This study is primarily concerned with the plight of child soldiers in northern Uganda and how their effective reintegration and rehabilitation (RR) could lead to successful peacebuilding. The study is premised on the hypothesis that `the promotion of the RR of former child soldiers by providing psychosocial support based on traditional and indigenous resources may contribute to conditions of peace and stability in northern Uganda. The main contribution of this research is that it explores the relevance of psychosocial support based on the traditional and indigenous resources to the RR of child soldiers and peacebuilding of war-torn societies. Psychosocial support based on traditional and indigenous resources as an element of peacebuilding has been the neglected element of peacebuilding by the liberal peacebuilding interventions in most war-torn societies. For example, while traditional and indigenous resources in northern Uganda have been instrumental in the RR of former child soldiers, most scholars and policy makers have largely paid attention to the usual official government and United Nations structured top-down interventions that emphasize Western approaches of peacebuilding. More so, the official approaches have tended to marginalize the plight of former child soldiers in the reconstruction and peacebuilding of northern Uganda. Yet, failing to pay sufficient attention to effective RR of child soldiers could undermine the peace dividends already achieved in northern Uganda. The study also analyses the limitations of psychosocial support based on traditional and indigenous resources in the RR of former child soldiers. It further examines why Western approaches of psychosocial support in the RR of child soldiers have remained in use in spite of the criticisms levelled against them. The study examines other peacebuilding interventions, both official and unofficial, that have been implemented in northern Uganda. The study establishes that traditional and indigenous resources are still popular and have been widely used in northern Uganda in the RR of child soldiers. Majority of former child soldiers who were interviewed observed that they found traditional and indigenous resources more helpful than the Western models of psychosocial support. However, it was also established that there is a significant section of former child soldiers who found Western models more relevant in their RR processes. Based on these findings, the study recommends an integrative and holistic model of psychosocial support that blends good elements from both traditional and indigenous resources and Western approaches with greater emphasis on the former. [Author Abstract]

6.)   **Baldwin, H.**

Fighting to survive in Rwanda: War, agency and victimhood.

Ph.D. dissertation, Boston College. 2006.

Within the literature on children and women in war zones, female child soldiers are consistently portrayed as victims. Traditionally, this label of victim has been in direct contrast to the concept of agency. However, with a broader definition of agency it becomes clear that even the most victimized individuals can and do display agency in their lives. This research examined the ways in which young women who participated in fighting forces in Rwanda expressed agency before, during, and after their experiences in the army. Using qualitative analysis of semi-structured interviews former adolescent soldiers in Rwanda, I found evidence of agency in four categories: the decision to join the army, the decision to leave the army, decisions regarding relationships, and the decision to take part in a sewing association. The findings are important because they help to reframe the way adolescents and women in war and post war zones are portrayed. One unintended effect of the current literature's focus on their status as victims may be to reduce the degree to which the adolescents and young women feel they have the power to improve their own lives. By focusing on their agency, researchers, policy makers, and those who work with adolescent female former child soldiers may also help them to believe in their ability to face future challenges in their lives. [Author Abstract]

7.)   **Barahona Martin, J.**

The juridical protection of children in armed conflicts.

M.A. thesis, Universidad de Huelva (Spain). 2002.

In recent armed conflicts, the civilian population, and particularly children, turn out to be the main victims. Does Public International Law offer any legal instruments to change that reality? This thesis, which tries to answer that question, is divided into an introductory chapter, three main chapters and a final part for conclusions. In the introductory chapter, a short evolution of Humanitarian Law is analysed together with Public International Law in general, to show how children deserve special treatment. Chapter I deals with two important terminological questions which affect the real protection of children in wars: the definition of a child and when an armed conflict qualifies as international or non-international. Chapter II is about the instruments to protect the child as a part of the civilian population and in their own right as civilian, and in Chapter III the particular problems and solutions for child soldiers are analysed. [Author Abstract]

8.) **Beirens, H. L. M. A.**

Voluntary child soldiering: a case-study of the anti-apartheid struggle.

Ph.D. dissertation, University of Warwick (United Kingdom). 2004.

In this thesis, I present a theoretical framework in which children's voluntary participation in armed conflict becomes a reasonable act within their social environment. I argue that in order to gain a more analytical understanding of why children volunteer, social scientists require an in-depth knowledge of the political, social and economic conditions in which they join up and of the meanings that children attach to those situations and their reactions. Prior quantitative data on the social distribution of child volunteering have often been used to proclaim that 'the most vulnerable of the vulnerable' are recruited. On the basis of a discourse analysis of UNHCR's policies and activities in relation to under-age recruitment, I illustrate my claim that dominant Euro-American conceptualisations of childhood have primarily shaped research and humanitarian aid regarding child soldiering and resulted in the portrayal of child soldiers as innocent victims who are corrupted by adult wars. I subsequently go on to show how a new paradigm for the study of childhood can enhance contemporary knowledge on the social processes and factors that lead children to consider and eventually join a military group or opt for an alternative mode of action to cope with their dire situation. In my qualitative case-study of child soldiering in the anti-apartheid struggle, I found that in joining a political organisation and subsequently its military wing, young South Africans sought to assert their (political) agency within the structural and cultural features that shaped their social environment. Within the context of changing peer and intergenerational relationships, these children carved out more powerful identities for them to address the social injustices that had affected their personal and collective lives. [Author Abstract]

9.) **Borisova, I. I.**

Child soldiers returning home from war: Family and caregiver impact on psychosocial reintegration.

Ed.D. dissertation, Harvard University. 2009.

Previous research with former child soldiers has documented varying psychosocial outcomes among this group of war-affected youth, suggesting that processes of protection and resilience are at play. However, not enough work has focused on building evidence around the active ingredients in such processes. The family presents a good opportunity for exploring protective variables that may exert a positive impact on the psychosocial adjustment of returning child soldiers. In my thesis, I used a variety of statistical methods, including Structural Equation Modeling, to explore the effects of three family-level variables on the adjustment outcomes of 286 former child combatants from Sierra Leone. Specifically, I was interested in the family placement of the child upon his/her return home, the socio-economic resources of the family with which the child was reunified, and the extent of caregiver knowledge of child experiences with violence during the war. Several findings are noteworthy. First, my research demonstrated that reunification with immediate family members seems beneficial for youth- the youth exhibited lower levels of internalizing problems and higher levels of positive outcomes as compared to their peers who were reunified with extended family members of foster parents. Second, contrary to the hypothesis that low socio-economic status would adversely affect youth, I found that youth in economically disadvantaged families exhibited lower levels of externalizing problems and higher levels of positive behaviors as compared to youth in well-to-do families. Gender did not appear to moderate the impact of family placement or SES. Finally, I found that caregiver's under-estimation of youth's perpetration of violence, as well as youth's direct experiences with violence, was associated with lower levels of prosocial attitudes and confidence/self agency among former child soldiers. On the other hand, caregiver's over-estimation of involvement in and perpetration of violence (often indicative of accurate caregiver reporting of such events) resulted in higher levels of positive behaviors and attitudes among adolescents. My findings highlight the importance of the family in the process of reintegration. In addition, they have implications for developing thoughtful intervention programs that consider the needs of the child in the context of the family with whom he/she is reunified. [Author Abstract]

10.) **Breau, J.**

The road to reintegration: Girl soldiers' journey in post-conflict Sierra Leone.

M.A. thesis, Dalhousie University (Canada). 2007.

While the international community has started to acknowledge the presence of child soldiers in contemporary armed conflicts and their specific needs in the war-to-peace transition, the particular circumstances surrounding girl soldiers' journey in post-conflict societies remain under-appreciated and misunderstood. This thesis seeks to understand the circumstances surrounding girl soldiers' low participation rate in the child-specific disarmament, demobilization and reintegration (DDR) programme as well as the strained relationship between former girl soldiers and their communities following Sierra Leone's 1991 to 2002 civil war. An appreciation for the experiences of Sierra Leone's girl soldiers may lead to developing better-suited policies to meet the special needs of girls related to gender and sex. Otherwise, a theoretical understanding of these girls' experiences speaks to the epistemological and normative implications of child-specific programming, specifically of the seeming incompatibility of the best policies for reintegration and the recognition of children's actual wartime experiences. [Author Abstract]

11.) **Brons, K. E.**

Assessing the innocence and victimization of child soldiers.

M.S. thesis, The University of Alabama. 2013.

To date, the majority stance taken by researchers in the field of criminology has been that child soldiers should be treated as innocent victims of war. While there have been some authors who have examined whether this label should be attached to the child, none have firmly taken the minority side in this debate. International law disregards the criminal acts against humanity committed by a child soldier and instead criminalizes the adults who either abducted the child for military duty or allowed the child to willingly volunteer for the armed services. This thesis proposes that many child soldiers are not innocent victims, but they are instead perpetrators of violence. In doing so, definitions of 'innocent' and 'victim' are called upon to show how many child soldiers are neither of these things and are able to take advantage of the International Criminal Court because of the ambiguity in international law. Labeling theory is used as the theoretical framework for this thesis. By labeling child soldiers as innocent victims, it has an adverse effect that allows child soldiers to continue committing criminal acts. [Author Abstract]

12.) **Brownell, G. E.**

The reintegration experiences of ex-child soldiers in Liberia.

Ph.D. dissertation, The University of Texas at Arlington. 2013.

Previous researchers have reported the lasting effects of child soldiering and the difficulties that ex-child soldiers experience as they transition to civilian living. The primary purpose of this study is to gain a better understanding about the reintegration experiences and meaning of reintegration as perceived by ex-child soldiers located in or near Monrovia, the capital city of Liberia. Furthermore, this study explores participants' expectations, perceptions of the reintegration process as well as contributing factors and obstacles to reintegration that helped shaped their reintegration experience within the context of Liberia. A phenomenological research design was used to study the reintegration experiences of 34 (20 males and 14 females) ex-child soldiers. Data analysis uncovered six textural themes: motivation for disarmament, desire to rebuild lives through knowledge and skills, dissatisfaction with reintegration, perceptions of reintegration, powerlessness and perception of future combat participation. It was concluded that participants in this study were influenced to disarm by external motivators, desired to rebuild their lives through knowledge and skills, were dissatisfied with reintegration, perceived themselves as not fully reintegrated, experienced powerlessness and were unwilling to return to future combat despite economic hardships. [Author Abstract]

13.) **Burnley, A. P.**

The human toll from African conflicts: Explaining conflict resources.

M.A. thesis, Webster University. 2009.

The purpose of this research is to determine the human toll exacted by conflict resources in political, border security and ethnic wars of Africa, (conflicts common in what Mary Kaldor of the London School of Economics has termed as new wars); have on the human toll; human toll being defined as the number of deaths and internally displaced people (IDP). The case-studies chosen establish with a high degree of accuracy that conflict may be sustained and more importantly prolonged when there is a source of wealth deemed worth exploiting. By understanding the relationship between conflict resources and the human toll in conflicts in which conflict resources are present, the root causes of a conflict may become easier to eliminate. I hypothesize wars (political, border security or ethnic) where conflict resources are in abundance produce a greater amount of human deaths and IDP (the human toll) in comparison to wars where conflict resources are not in abundance, because their duration is prolonged due to the exploitation of resources and the cycle of violence it produces. Intra- and inter-state conflicts in Angola, the Democratic Republic of Congo (DRC) and Sudan, are grouped into specific categories of political, border security and ethnic conflicts as case studies using Causal/Comparative research to explain the findings regarding the human toll in these conflicts. Furthermore, the presence of conflict resources in these conflicts separated Angola, the DRC and Sudan from the other wars within their categorical grouping. The conflicts described above in which conflict resources were present were longer than those without conflict resources. However, though conflict resources may potentially be a cause of conflicts being prolonged, the conflicts in which they were present did not sufficiently show a greater human toll incurred when compared to these in which conflict resources were not present. The strength of this research adds to studies of new wars, conflict resources, deaths, IDP and/or instability in Africa. Unfortunately, this study does not factor in other possible aspects of human toll; such as the countless number of women and children who have been victims of rape or mutilation, nor the many child soldiers whose lives have been destroyed by these conflicts. [Author Abstract]

14.) **Connolly Black, H.**

Forgiveness: The cultural implications for Ugandan child soldiers: A qualitative exploration of the benefits and consequences of culturally-advocated forgiveness for Ugandan child soldiers post abduction.

Psy.D. dissertation, Azusa Pacific University. 2013.

This study considers forgiveness concurrent with the reunification of child soldiers post abduction by the LRA, led by rebel leader Joseph Kony. Focusing on the Acholi tribe in Northern Uganda, this project examined the reunification process of the child soldier through the culturally nuanced variable of forgiveness. Reunification extends to nuclear family, tribe, and peer group. The 24 participants for the qualitative sample are composed of female and male adolescent child soldiers between the ages of 14 to 18 years. All participants were members of the Acholi tribe from The Village of Hope Orphanage (VOH) in Gulu, Uganda. This study addressed the research gaps in the final chapter of the abduction cycle. Examining the individual, psychosocial, neurological, and cultural implications of reunification aided by the inclusion of culturally promoted forgiveness, the endeavor sought to gather data to classify the necessity and efficacy of forgiveness in a post-conflict environment. [Author Abstract]

15.)   **Davis, J. A.**

Demobilizing the Minors: Examining Compliance with International Child Soldiering Laws.

Ph.D. dissertation, The George Washington University. 2011.

Why do some states follow international laws prohibiting the use of child soldiers, while others do not? While child soldiering is something that most states have avoided throughout history, recent trends indicate this is changing; in 2005, more than 40 percent of all armed organizations around the world employed children under 18 as soldiers. In light of this increase in use of children as soldiers, international law has codified a series of prohibitions and conventions against the use of child soldiers. In some cases, these laws have had considerable impact; some of the governments who used child soldiers have ceased, and returned to using only adults. Others claim to have stopped using child soldiers, but found ways to co-opt rebel groups who continue using children to fight their wars.

Yet other groups or states have continued using child soldiers in spite of the dictates of international law. This creates an intriguing puzzle for social scientists; why do some states change practices to conform to international laws against child soldiering, while others ignore these laws and continue recruiting children? This dissertation examined compliance patterns in Burma, Senegal, Uganda, Sri Lanka, Colombia, and Rwanda to provide insights on the reasons why states choose to comply with or disregard international child soldiering laws. [Author Abstract]

16.) **Davis, M.**

Children: The new face of war.

M.A. thesis, California State University,

Dominguez Hills. 2010.

The twentieth century was fraught with carnage from numerous wars. They had varying causes and results, but one aspect of war that is gaining attention in the West is the use of children in combat. Child soldiers, some as young as eight years old, bring a completely new face to warfare. In addition, having children fight for one's cause also produces a new set of traumas to survivors of war: to the soldier fighting against the child and especially to the child combatants. As the United States continues to wage war in Iraq and Afghanistan and persists in contributing armed forces to other international conflicts, American soldiers continue to encounter children either as foe or as comrade. The intent of this thesis is to compile current information on children in warfare by looking at causes for the use of child soldiers, the training involved in making a child into a soldier, and the effects of this transformation on the child and the community. In addition, two case studies from Africa--Sierra Leone and Uganda--are used to show examples of child soldiers' experiences. In addition to scholarly studies on these countries in which children have been used as soldiers, children's memoirs and testimonies are be utilized to show the very personal side of this tragedy. [Author Abstract]

17.)   **Falcon, S. M.**

Victims or criminals? The effects of the media on the public perception of the role of children in the Mexican drug war.

M.A. thesis, The University of Texas at El Paso. 2013.

With the evolution of war, new international norms have been created. Boys were once groomed for war, but the laws of today aim to protect children. I address the issue of the role of children as victims or criminals to the ongoing violence of the war on drugs in Mexico. I look at the different international conventions where children's rights are defined, and whether they can be held responsible for their actions during times of war. I hypothesize that the framing of media coverage affects the public perception of children involved in this conflict, in regards to their core beliefs through which they interpret the media and the negativity bias; public opinion will be a result of how the media depicts these children. I analyze news articles, from both sides of the border, to determine whether the actions of children are framed in a positive or negative context. I conduct an experiment with University of Texas at El Paso students, in which I provide mock news articles that intentionally frame the actions of children in a positive and negative context. I analyze the pre-test and post-test in order to find support for my hypothesis that framing of the media affects the public perception of the role that children are playing. By contributing to prior research on child soldiers, this study demonstrates that the term child soldier can apply to unconventional war; the War on Drugs, a concept. This research project opens the door for further studies to analyze the role of child soldiers in unconventional wars. [Author Abstract]

18.)   **Farsad, N.**

How to reintegrate former girl soldiers in African countries back to their societies.

M.A. thesis, University of Alberta (Canada). 2010.

Studies show that 40 percent of existing child soldiers are girls. In order to make and sustain peace in war-affected countries, it is important to ensure that all members of a community, including women and girls, are reintegrated successfully. Failure of successful reintegration of former girl soldiers may result in a collapse back into war. This research attempts to find current gaps in reintegration programs for girl combatants. Numerous research papers, related articles, and filed studies have been consulted. This thesis proposes that women involved in rebel forces are a microcosm of what is happening in society. Therefore, in order to have a successful reintegration program, it is important to receive direct feedback from these girls so the programs can be implemented successfully in the society. [Author Abstract]

19.)   **Heninger, L.**

Conducting qualitative research in countries at war: Implementation and impact factors in a study of girls in armed groups.

Ph.D. dissertation, City University of New York. 2005.

This study seeks to describe the qualitative research methodology employed in the study entitled "The Voices of Girl Child Soldiers," to contrast it with the qualitative research literature in social work, and to consider it in the light of reflective theory. Put simply, it is a study of a study. Utilizing a comparative case study approach it draws on research team experiences in the four countries that served as sites in the original study (N = 4). In total, 15 interviews were conducted with team members in all four countries and with the Principal Investigator of the original study. Thirteen of the interviews took place in person and in country, two were telephone interviews. Interview guides for the current study were developed from a review of the literature on qualitative research methodology and from notes and experiences derived from the original study. Notes on the process of "dialogues on methodology" conducted with research team members during the original study, recorded personal reflections during and after the dialogues, materials for the dialogues, and the final reports of the original study were reviewed for the current study. Despite exploration of social work and social science literature on qualitative methodology, it did not offer a fully effective way to implement a flexible and culturally nuanced approach to research with children in situations of violent conflict. To determine the gaps in the qualitative methodologies utilized in the research literature pertaining to children in situations of violent conflict, the specifics of the methodology of the girl soldier study were contrasted with existing literature, and considered through the lens of reflective theory. Data analysis indicated an intersection between the categories of implementation of the method of research and the impacts of the implementation of the study on both the research team members and the girls they interviewed. Reflective theory provided a way to understand the changes that occurred in the original study, both methodological and individual. This intersection generated a framework for study design, implementation, and follow-up that may be useful in qualitative researchers in future cross-cultural studies of children in situations of violent conflict. [Author Abstract]

20.)   **Hynes, B.**

Children of the borderlands: Young soldiers in the reproduction of warfare.

Ph.D. dissertation, University of Denver. 2008.

This study considers the intersection of locality with international security through the lens of one of the larger manpower drivers of recent African wars--child soldiers. Local norms and networks in child soldiering illuminate two aspects of international security--the problem of war contagion and the challenges of international regime efficacy. First, is the relationship between local capabilities and the expansion of war. In sub-Saharan Africa, regional conflict and child soldiering are intertwined. A theoretical concern with porous borders and weak states contends the role of locality can serve as a stimulus and momentum for expanding war. This study compares the border regions of the Namibian Kavango with the Mano River and Kailahun regions of Sierra Leone as war began to cross over from Angola and Liberia, respectively. It dissects local configurations and finds that border localities are not endemically dangerous. Instead, expected and unexpected pathways of local action can make a difference in both in the degree of war's spread and the extent of children's participation. Second, what could be called a global anti-child soldiering regime, an international configuration strongly linked to the protection-based theoretic in human security, emerged and flourished over the past 15 years. Programmatic actions against child soldiering, accompanied by international legal norms shunning child soldiering, have escalated dramatically. Yet, international estimates of child soldiers active in combat did not diminish. On the contrary, child soldiering grew from 250,000 children a year in 1998, to more than 300,000 in 2005. Why haven't these actions halted child soldiering growth? In the details of local involvement and resistance to cross-border child soldiering, distinct gaps between the conceptual and substantive factors of import in prevention locally, and those stressed by anti-child soldier networks globally, come to light. The findings in this study provide needed political specificity for the human security literature and the global anti-child soldiering regime. The concrete conditions and localized ideas where efforts to thwart child soldiering have had some success (Namibia) and where they have not (Sierra Leone) concretize human security through the concept of capabilities, for use in conflict zones. A framework for evaluating conflict conditions, and an analytic for targeted support to elements that push away from violent involvement on the whole--and involvement of children specifically-- flow from the study's findings. [Author Abstract]

21.)   **Jevtic, E.**

Achieving rehabilitation and reintegration of children associated with armed groups.
Ph.D. dissertation, University of Kent at Canterbury (United Kingdom). 2010.

The aim of this thesis is to critically reflect on the implementation feasibility of guidelines recently developed by the UN and its affiliated programs and funds, and their ability to provide long-term solutions for rehabilitation and reintegration of children associated with armed groups. Building on Jareg's reintegration theory, the thesis claims that solutions toward rehabilitation and reintegration can be initiated through the application of international guidelines and recommendations designed to help programs strengthen relationships with the family and the community, provide education, health and gender initiatives as part of psychosocial heating. To validate the claim, thesis sets up the analysis method by identifying five main documents (*Machel Report, Cape Town*

Principles, Paris Principles, Integrated Disarmament, Demobilization and Reintegration Standards and *the Machel +10 Report)* which specifically provide guidance and recommendations to address rehabilitation and reintegration of child soldiers. By extracting and grouping their recommendations, the thesis develops a RR guidelines working list, which is applied in the individual and comparative analysis of the two case studies, *Give me a Chance (GMAC)* in northern Uganda and *Communauté des Eglises de Pentecôte en Afrique Centrale (CEPAC)* in the eastern Democratic Republic of the Congo (DRC). With the help of the RR guidelines working list, thesis conducts validation of Jareg's reintegration theory. In addition, the comparative analysis leads to recognition of recommendations; specific strengths and weaknesses, confirming their applicability to assist rehabilitation and reintegration of child soldiers. [Author Abstract]

22.)   **Jones, L.**

The Marginalization of Girl Soldiers in Sierra Leone's Disarmament, Demobilization and Reintegration Program: An analysis based on structuration theory.

M.S.W. thesis, McGill University (Canada). 2008.

An estimated 48,000 child soldiers were involved in the violent civil war in Sierra Leone between 1991 and 2002. It is suggested that approximately 12,000 were girls. Lacking material possessions and facing other negative structural factors, the majority was in need of some form of assistance post-conflict. Although international aid response was substantial, only 500 girls entered the countrywide Disarmament, Demobilization and Reintegration (DDR) program. The remainder followed a variety of different courses. Giddens' structuration theory offers a useful theoretical framework to explore the reasons for their absence in the program, as it permits a focus on the role of structure and agency in understanding behaviour. Social stigmatization and a gender-biased DDR program, within a broader structure of gender inequality, are identified as the principal problems. [Author Abstract]

23.) **Keah, M. K.**

Rehabilitating child soldiers and war-affected children in western Africa: A study.

M.Sc. thesis, University of Guelph (Canada). 2003.

This study examined the effectiveness of institutional rehabilitation programs such as the Post Traumatic Stress Disorder (PTSD) method of de-traumatizing in West Africa and also non-institutional or community approach to rehabilitation. The study further enhances the understanding of how governments, international and local NGOs as well as United Nations organizations can best rehabilitate child soldiers in West Africa and possibly elsewhere. This study is of particular importance to policy makers in the above named agencies. Data were gathered through interviews, questionnaires and participant observations. The results indicated that little effect is made on child soldiers who undergo PTSD programs, though this statement is made with caution due to the limited number of children that were involved in this study, thereby making it a qualitative rather than a quantitative study. The study revealed that institutional rehabilitation may not be the best way of rehabilitation for child soldiers and war-affected children in community oriented regions. However, the study does not suggest that institutional rehabilitation is unsuitable for communities in West Africa and should be done with, rather, it suggests that in order to get better results from rehabilitating children in community oriented regions such as West Africa and improve other issues such as human security, there should be some combination of both institutional and non-institutional efforts. [Author Abstract]

24.)   **Kleinfeld, M.**

Depoliticizing space in Sri Lanka: The discursive utility of the child during times of war.

Ph.D. dissertation, University of Kentucky. 2005.

This research investigates the role of tropes of the child in the politicization and depoliticization of national spaces during the Sri Lankan civil war in two case studies. The first case examines the production of humanitarian space in Sri Lanka in the form of annual ceasefires for children called "Days of Tranquility" (DOTS). The DOTS were designed to create temporary nonpolitical spaces in support of "National Immunization Days" (NIDs), an immunization strategy conducted as part of the global Polio Eradication Initiative (PEI). The second case investigates political discourse associated with underage military recruitment (i.e. child soldiers). A variety of ethnographic techniques were employed during fieldwork in Sri Lanka from August 2001 to July 2002, including participant observation, semi-structured interviewing, and document compilation. Approximately 60 in depth interviews were conducted with United Nations agencies staff, Sri Lankan government officials and those working for international and national non-governmental organizations. Observations from the 2001 DOTS at three Sri Lankan sites between September and October 2001 were also chronicled. The examples in the dissertation provide ample evidence that tropes of the child are particularly effective at enhancing or diminishing political legitimacy. The case of the DOTs demonstrates that actors supporting nonpolitical humanitarian spaces can represent themselves as morally fit to govern even where there is scant evidence that nonpolitical spaces are actually produced. Child soldier narratives demonstrate the power of child tropes to stigmatize and shame political actors. In both of these cases, international organizations that advocate for global child rights provide a critical link between internal conflict and domestic political actors, and international public opinion. This research provides original material on the construction of humanitarian space, particularly as a space of diverse organizational interrelations as well as the goals set by individual actors and in combination. This analysis will contribute to ongoing debates within political geographic and international relations literatures concerned with territorial sovereignty, humanitarian actors and spaces, and transnational relations. In addition, by examining the political significance of conceptions of children in modern life, this project contributes to scholarship on children and geography, as well as children in cross-cultural perspective. [Author Abstract]

25.)   **Kohrt, B. A.**

Political violence and mental health in Nepal: War in context, structural violence, and the erasure of history.

Ph.D. dissertation, Emory University. 2009.

The experience of war can have immediate and long-term consequences for the mental health of women, men, and children. Exposure to war and other forms of political violence typically occur against a backdrop of structural violence, which marginalizes populations and is a risk factor for poor mental health. The goal in this dissertation is to examine the effects of the People's War in Nepal on mental health taking into account the history of structural violence threats to mental health including caste-based and gender discrimination, poverty, and the exploitation and abuse of children. Methods drawn from anthropology, epidemiology, genetics, and endocrinology were employed to study two war-affected populations: civilian adults in a rural community and child soldiers. A three-component conceptual framework was developed to assess and model mental health: (1) War in context evaluates risk factors according to prewar, wartime, and postwar exposures; (2) Vulnerability refers to person-culture and gene-environment interactions which increase the risk of mental health problems; (3) Heterogeneity of outcomes demonstrates the need to examine a range of psychiatric and local categories of suffering as well as impaired functioning. Ethnopsychology-based models are especially important to address stigma in psychosocial interventions for war-affected children and adults. This conceptual framework fosters research and intervention that addresses war in the broader context of experience and prevents the erasure of history risked when exclusively investigating or treating war-related trauma. [Author Abstract]

26.)   **Korula, A. R.**

The protection of children in armed conflict. The implementation of human rights regimes: an empirical study of children associated with fighting forces.

Ph.D. dissertation, University of Exeter (United Kingdom). 2008.

This dissertation examines the issues and problems associated with the protection of children in the context of armed conflict, particularly child soldiers (CS) and children associated with fighting forces (CAFF). It assesses, through examination of a Liberian case study, whether implementation is effective in applicable human rights regimes (HRRs), and whether they are adequate measures of child protection. The context in which the protection of children in armed conflict is considered is set out, namely HRRs, as evident in post-conflict peacebuilding, democratic governance and development. Their characteristics and workings are described, and a classification developed.

The key actors are then identified and their varying types of commitment classified. To assess the implementation and effectiveness of HRRs, selected implementation review mechanisms, both formal and informal, are also examined. In describing specific relevant and inter-related HRRs, the complexity of these regimes and the synergies between them are brought to light. In doing so, some of the issues and problems compounding or confounding implementation at the universal, regional and national levels are also highlighted. In the case study of Liberia, West Africa, the implementation and effectiveness of HRRs, as well as other relevant and related regimes are examined at the national and local levels, with consideration given to some of the interventions implemented by international organizations engaging in peacebuilding. The reintegration and rehabilitation of CAFF is then described with reference to a community in Central Liberia, whose approach to implementation of the relevant HRRs appears to be exemplary and may even be replicable. Insights derived from the Liberian case have policy implications; they highlight shifts required at the local, national, regional or universal levels for implementation to be more effective and durable. Some areas for further research are also delineated. [Author Abstract]

27.)   **Krech, R. J.**

The reintegration of former child combatants: A case study of NGO programming in Sierra Leone. M.A. thesis, University of Toronto (Canada). 2003.

This thesis explores the reintegration programmes of World Vision Sierra Leone for former child combatants in Sierra Leone. Using a social model of discourse that conceptually draws on Michel Foucault and Nancy Fraser, this study analyzes World Vision's programming in the context of its relationships with UNICEF and CIDA's Peacebuilding Unit, as well as other Sierra Leonean governmental bodies. The aim of this thesis is to describe why World Vision Sierra Leone identifies the reintegration needs of former child soldiers as it does in the context of post-conflict peacebuilding in Sierra Leone's complex emergency. [Author Abstract]

28.) **Lasley, T. C.**

Creed vs. deed: Secession, legitimacy and the use of child soldiers.

Ph.D. dissertation, University of Kentucky. 2012.

The use of child soldiers has troubled human rights activists, policy-makers, and local communities for decades. Although rebellions around the world routinely use children in their activities, many do not. Despite its overwhelming importance for conflict resolution, the topic of child soldiers remains understudied. My research blends classic rational choice and constructivist themes to develop an explanation for when child soldiers will be used, and when they will be avoided. The likelihood of child recruitment is influenced by the value of international opinion; this is determined by the groups' long-term goals. Secessionist rebellions desire to have their own state. However, statehood is jealously guarded by the international community and is only granted under extreme circumstances. The use of child soldiers has been condemned around the world as a crime against humanity, and it can curtail international support. Thus, secessionists should be the least likely rebel type to use child soldiers out of a concern to appear legitimate. Opportunistic rebellions face few constraints in their recruitment efforts. They do not desire international support because their long-term goal is the same as their short term goal: profit. Instead of refraining from using children in order to curry favor with external parties, they will abduct, adopt, and abuse children because they are cheaper to employ than adults. Opportunists are unconcerned with losing legitimacy or reducing the chances of victory. Therefore, they should be the most likely to use child soldiers. Concern for costs can affect all rebels. As duration grows, constraints over long-term legitimacy diminish. Therefore, all rebellions should be more likely to use child soldiers as duration increases. I test my theory quantitatively by looking at 103 rebel groups active between 1998-2008. I explore rebellions in Somalia, Colombia, Afghanistan and Sudan to further elucidate the causal mechanisms. There is considerable empirical support for the theory. These results offer policy-relevant conclusions in the areas of rehabilitation and conflict resolution. More importantly, they offer a workable strategy to curb the use of child soldiers in civil war. [Author Abstract]

29.)   **Madden, C.**

Boko Haram: Children as weapons of war.
M.S. thesis, Utica College. 2014.

The purpose of this research was to identify children used as weapons of war and terrorism through acts by Nigerian radical Muslim group Boko Haram. The matter of child weapons posed significance in the fight against terrorism. Historically, child weapons faced warfare but in different venues than terrorism sought to exploit them. Throughout time, child soldiers fought on the battlefield or used for pleasure and race dilution through sexual violence. Terrorist acts by Boko Harm sought to use children as human shields. Often terrorism focused on the shock value and emotional impact rather than the intent to win in tradition warfare. Boko Hara was not alone in using children as weapons of war during the conflicts in Nigeria. Police brutality against the youth of Nigeria generated opposition in the form of spin-off Muslim youth groups. In addition, a corrupt Nigerian government inhibited equal education angering the youth fueling the already injured psyche of Nigerian children into adult terrorist organizations. The problem of child weapons in Nigeria roots back to corrupted educational and governmental systems. The poor example called the state of Nigeria taught youth that violence solved problems and oppression strengthened leadership. It was no wonder the children of Nigeria once abused by their own grew up to be terrorists. The answer to this problem, outlined by the United Nations guidelines on war crimes against children, requires an upholding of Geneva Convention and UN rules by those with an interest in Nigeria. [Author Abstract]

30.)   **Martin, A.**

Exploring the reintegration process for child soldiers: A case study of young women and their children in northern Uganda.

M.S.W. thesis, Wilfrid Laurier University (Canada). 2009.

Child soldiering has occurred throughout history in the never-ending battle over land, resources and human rights. The earliest mention of minors in war comes from antiquity however it was not until the 1970s that the first international convention came into effect in an attempt to limit the participation of children in armed conflict (Wikipedia, 2009b). Unfortunately, children remain active in armed conflicts around the world as combatants, porters, spies, messengers, sex slaves and human shields. Human Rights Watch (2007) estimates that 200,000 to 300,000 children are currently serving in rebel and government forces in over 20 countries around the world. One of these current conflicts is the civil war, turned regional conflict, between the Lord's Resistance Army (LRA) and the Ugandan military. This 23 year conflict has received much international attention due to the notoriety of the LRA's brutality against the civilian population and the abduction of children into its ranks as combatants and 'sex slaves'. With hundreds of non-governmental organizations (NGOs) in northern Uganda to assist civilians in general, and former child soldiers in particular, it is amazing to discover the limited impact they are actually having on the situation. Young women returning from the LRA with children appear to be a particularly vulnerable demographic in this context (McKay, 2004). The literature asserts that these individuals face more difficulty upon their return to society and remain invisible in research and practice. As such, this thesis sets out to understand the experiences of these girls and young women within the rebel army as well as upon their return to family and community. Fourteen participants were interviewed by the researcher with diverse backgrounds including:

academics, researchers, child protection workers, and two Ugandans who are of Acholi ethnicity, the primary group targeted and affected by this conflict. An additional thirteen transcripts were provided by another researcher based on interviews she conducted with women who had returned home with children from the LRA. The major findings and contribution to the literature include the very different experiences of girls and young women based upon where they were taken. Individuals taken to LRA bases in Sudan lead a more normalized existence as compared to girls and young women who remained in Uganda. Many of these individuals return to their communities with skills and strengths that could easily be adapted to benefit the larger society and yet are not being tapped into and utilized. Instead, NGOs continue to employ universal or 'cookie-cutter' approaches which have very limited impact. Reception centres for these children and youth are beneficial in the sense that they provide shelter and cursory attempts at normalizing their behavior. However, these centres, which exist to ease the transition back into society, run the very high risk of doing quite the opposite; of creating dependency and further disempowering members of the community. This thesis describes the experiences of girls and young women within Acholi culture, within the LRA, and upon return to their families and communities; offers a critical look at NGOs working with these individuals; and provides suggestions and recommendations on how to improve upon successful outcomes for former female child soldiers. [Author Abstract]

31.) **Massey, C. M.**

Child soldiers - theory and reality of their existence: the question of international protection available to them in contemporary times.

Ph.D. dissertation, The University of Nottingham (United Kingdom). 2001.

Children are regarded as holders of specific rights and special privileges, and yet more and more children continue to be abused in one form or the another. One of the worst forms of abuse is the willingness of adults today to use children on the numerous frontlines of the world. This aim of this thesis is to develop an argument against the practice of child recruitment and participation and for the practice of non-recruitment and hence non-participation in any form of all children under 18 in armed conflicts. Chapter One introduces the problem, it reflects on the impact and effect of armed conflict on Children, Chapters Two and Three present the moral arguments and the legal basis for extending protection to children from this form of abuse. Chapters Four and Five considers the issues of recruitment and subsequent treatment on capture for these child soldiers. Chapter Six is a case study of Uganda. This case study attempts to answer questions that might help in reaching out realistically to help children in this situation. Chapter Seven emphasises on the right to rehabilitation. Chapter Eight analyses the response of the international Community to the problem of Child Soldiers and Chapter Nine in the form of concluding remarks summaries the conclusions of this thesis, that it is possible to stop this practice but we need a stronger and united political stand for this purpose. It presses for the adoption and enforcement of an Optional Protocol to the Convention on the Rights of the Child which will establish a flat ban on all forms of participation by all children under 18. [Author Abstract]

32.)   **Maulden, P. A.**

Former child soldiers and sustainable peace processes: Demilitarizing the body, heart, and mind.

Ph.D. dissertation, George Mason University. 2007.

This dissertation explores theory and practice in post-conflict demobilization, rehabilitation, and reintegration programs for former child soldiers in the country cases of Sierra Leone, Colombia, and Mozambique. The study examines aspects of war and violence as they impact socio-cultural norms, values, and practices, focusing on how individuals and groups interact with violence and how that interaction alters individual and group norms, values, and practices as a result. This process, termed social militarization, can lead to violence becoming a regular component of socialization. When this occurs, particularly in a context of protracted social conflict or civil war, children and youth use their agency to make sense of their environment and their options. In many cases, these young people enter the adult world of violence and gain, for the first time in their lives, the power and resources previously denied them. Moving from child responsibilities to those of the adult through violence is posited as adult/child domain shifts. When the fighting stops, former child soldiers are expected to shift out of the adult and violent domain and re-enter the nonviolent world of the child. The peace processes aimed at child soldiers take this as their main task. The young people must then learn to reorganize themselves and their actions around peaceful norms, values, and practices, termed in the study social demilitarization. Field research in Sierra Leone examined how well programs assist children and youth in this goal, detailed some of the problems faced by the young in the post-conflict environment, and suggested alternatives that could give these individuals power and agency through peaceful strategies. The underlying tensions between the categories of child, youth, and adult--in times of war and in times of peace--are examined throughout the text. The country cases serve to highlight the theories of protracted social conflict, social militarization, and adult/child domain shifts. The ongoing post-conflict construction of peace as more than just not war underscores the difficulties faced by former child soldiers as they struggle to demilitarize the body, heart, and mind in uncertain, and often unforgiving, circumstances. [Author Abstract]

33.)   **Messay, M.**

Unlocking the voices of child soldiers in sub-Saharan African novels, films and autobiographies.

Ph.D. dissertation, The Florida State University. 2014.

In this dissertation, I examine a variety of Francophone African novels, films, and autobiographies with female and male child-soldiers as main characters. My corpus includes well-known works such as Johnny Mad Dog by Emmanuel Dongola, Allah n'est pas obligé by Ahmadou Kourouma and Ezra by Newton Aduaka, as well as lesser-known works such as Les Anges Cannibales by Jean-Claude Derey and J'étais enfant-soldat by Lucien Badjoko. After explaining the phenomenon, the identity of child soldiers and my use of trauma theory in my introduction, I dedicate a chapter to each medium. In my analysis of the fictional works, I demonstrate how the writers use textual techniques such as intertextuality, repetition, alternating narrators and repetition in order to situate the creation of child soldiers, their trauma and violence in its historical, political and socio-cultural context. I also reveal how these works underscore the need to transmit the child soldier's story orally and textually. In my analysis of cinematic works, I examine how the filmmakers use cinematic techniques such as contrasting spaces to expose the child soldier's horrific experience and its damaging effects on the child and the community, and to transform the spectator into a witness to the child soldier's trauma and violence. In my last chapter, I examine how former child soldiers use their works to exorcise their trauma and draw attention to the real life difficulties linked to the phenomenon such as the difficulties that demobilized child soldiers face and our own ethical viewing and response to the trauma and violence of the child soldier. This dissertation will demonstrate how all these works accord a voice to the child soldier (in their witnessing of his/her traumatic and violent experiences) and offer invaluable insight into the phenomenon and its implications in Sub-Saharan Africa. [Author Abstract]

34.)   **Millard, A. S.**

*The reintegration of child soldiers after civil war:
an analysis with special reference to El Salvador
and Mozambique.*
Ph.D. dissertation, University of Bradford (United
Kingdom). 1999.

This thesis explores the question of child soldier
reintegration in post civil war environments.
Current views on the child soldier issue in the
academic literature are examined. The different
responses to the child soldier problem by
governments, international organisations or
NGOs are then delineated, and the gap between
the post-settlement needs of child soldiers and
the existent responses outlined. In order to
bridge this gap, a conflict resolution approach is
adopted, first, to highlight the nature of
contemporary conflicts which perpetuate the
child soldier phenomenon, and second, to
provide an interpretative context for post-war
reconstruction efforts. So far as concerns the
latter, particular attention is paid to the

experience of UN-brokered peace-settlement and post-settlement peace-building efforts. In short, this thesis attempts to bridge the discrepancies between existing programs and the needs of child soldiers in post-settlement environments in order to help to achieve a more adequate reintegration of child soldiers into civilian life. Although this research examines the child soldier reintegration problematique generally, special reference to child soldier post-settlement reconstruction experiences in El Salvador and Mozambique are made, and extensive fieldwork in both countries serves to illuminate the nature of the challenge of child soldier reintegration in different countries. [Author Abstract]

35.) **Murphy, C. E.**

Phenomenological Analysis of the Experiences of Former Child Soldiers from Africa.

Psy.D. dissertation, Massachusetts School of Professional Psychology. 2011.

The purpose of this study is to assess the experiences of former child soldiers during their membership as children in armed forces in Africa, as well as their experiences post-demobilization. Many children across the world continue to fight in these wars, violating their human rights for protection. These children are forced to commit and witness atrocities and are exposed to significant traumas throughout their participation in these groups. Efforts are made by many organizations and within many government policies to disarm, demobilize, and rehabilitate these individuals, with a goal of reintegrating them back into society. This study will aim to look at the experience of former child soldiers who have written autobiographies about their experiences. My method is a qualitative, phenomenological study in which four child soldier's autobiographies will be reviewed and coded for themes. After identifying themes, a model exemplifying these experiences will be formed. The results demonstrate that the following master themes: pre-war experiences, factors contributing to enlistment and ongoing service, survival mechanisms, and rehabilitation and intervention attempts were key aspects of the authors experiences. Subthemes such as loss, pain, post-traumatic stress, fear, faith, and emotional suppression provided insight into each author's experiences. These were established from the identification of keywords used throughout the text in great frequency, supporting these themes. In this paper quotations that led to the original formation of the themes were presented. This study demonstrated that despite similar circumstances each individual has their own unique perspective and story of engagement. It demonstrated further that interacting themes impacted their behavior and internal experiences of the war, as well as their rehabilitation experiences. This study illuminated area for future research that would help to gain a fuller understanding of the overall experiences of former child soldiers. [Author Abstract]

36.)   **Ochen, E.**

An exposition of intra-bush and post-bush experiences of formerly abducted child mothers in northern Uganda: issues in rehabilitation, resettlement and reintegration.

Ph.D. dissertation, University of Huddersfield (United Kingdom). 2011.

This qualitative study explores the intra-bush and post-bush experiences of formerly abducted child mothers (FACM) in Northern Uganda. Critical events in the lives of young women who were abducted as young girls to join rebel soldiers in the recent civil war are examined. These critical events include sexual violation, training and participation in battles as child soldiers, motherhood, intra-bush trauma and, escape or release. The study also explores how the young women coped with life in the post-bush society they had rejoined. I examine approaches, resources and opportunities for the rehabilitation of returning FACM, their resettlement process and reintegration. The methodology borrows from narrative analysis, phenomenology and grounded theory with the main methods being in-depth interviews with FACM and key informants as well as focus groups with community members and agency staff. Structuration theory, African feminist theories, child rights discourse and a conceptual framework focusing on rehabilitation, resettlement and reintegration are utilized as lenses through which the experiences of the young women are viewed. Findings suggest that while the FACM demonstrated considerable agency in managing the challenges they came across both in the bush and in the post-bush periods, this agency was significantly curtailed by social structures. The young women`s experiences, both in captivity and post-captivity were influenced by structural factors which were embedded within social systems and relationships. These factors formed the context for the lived realities of the young women which were in turn impacted by gender and culture. The FACM had to assume a multiplicity of roles and identities as girls, mothers, wives', fighters, which interconnected with individual agency. This contributed to the strengths and resilience the young women possessed and also led to non-compliance with traditional cultural practices in some instances making reintegration more difficult. The main contributions of the study are: in its demonstration that some African cultural traditions have points of convergence with the promotion of children rights; in increasing understanding of the role of patriarchal and matriarchal power in social life; and in the revelation of the agency of the young women and their resistance to structural violence, although this agency was not adequate for protection from abuse. The study isolates not only individual but social agency which can be utilized to support rehabilitation, resettlement and reintegration planning. It raises the significance of the quality of personal relationships in carrying out interventions for FACM, sheds lights on the issues surrounding social rejection of the young women, where this occurs, and argues for interventions that build on their strengths and considers not only post-bush but intra-bush experiences. [Author Abstract]

37.)   **Oliver, J.**

Promoting reintegration and building peace? An examination of education assistance for former child soldiers in northern Uganda.

M.A. thesis, Carleton University (Canada). 2010.

A wealth of policy and academic literature recommends education to support the reintegration of former child soldiers. However, very little methodologically rigorous research has examined the relationship between education and reintegration outcomes. This study uses process tracing to examine the impact of education assistance on reintegration while considering political, social, and economic factors and other intervening variables. Four related hypotheses are investigated. H1: Education supports the reintegration of former child soldiers. H2: While ex-combatant girls are more likely to experience stigma and difficulty reintegrating than ex-combatant boys, education supports the reintegration of both girls and boys. H3: Targeted education assistance supports reintegration. H4: Targeted education assistance increases stigma and inhibits reintegration. A single case study of northern Uganda was conducted to examine these hypotheses based on a review of the literature on reintegration and education, field interviews, and the population-based I (SWAY I 2006, SWAY II 2008). [Author Abstract]

38.)   **Oloya, O.**

Becoming a child soldier: A cultural perspective from autobiographical voices.

Ph.D. dissertation, York University (Canada). 2010.

What happens when children are forced to become child soldiers? How are they transformed from children to combatants? What role does culture play in how children become and remain combatants? The purpose of this dissertation is to address the above questions by exploring how Acholi children abducted by the rebel group the Lord's Resistance Army (LRM/A) in northern Uganda become child combatants. Using non-fictional autobiographical voices of child combatants, it explores how the competencies and disposition the children acquired through environmental and cultural backgrounds enhance their desirability for forced recruitment. Employing the theory which I term liminal repurposing of culture, I investigate how Acholi village children abducted by the LRM/A are forced to undergo specific manipulations of Acholi culture, and are subsequently transformed into child combatants. The main thrust of the study is grounded in the belief that Acholi children in rural northern Uganda are closely attached to their families and communities for physical, emotional and psychological development. After being abducted by the LRM/A and forced to undergo the process of transformation to become combatants, these children seek to restore some normalcy in their lives. They find sense of family and community within the repurposed culture of violence provided by the rebel force. Despite the violence of war, the child combatants develop a strong sense of loyalty to their substitute families within the rebel outfit. Key words: child combatant, violence, autobiographical voice, resilience, ethnocultural conflict, cultural devastation, cultural trauma [Author Abstract]

39.) **Owusu, V.**

The impact of child labor and child soldiers on economic development in Africa.

M.P.A. thesis, Arkansas State University. 2012.

Child soldiers and child labor contribute to extreme poverty, lack of education, shortage of human resources, and lack of parental or family guidance in many countries. More importantly, economic and educational impacts from child labor are widespread and persistent in many countries. In countries that are already poor, war tends to deteriorate economic and social conditions, thereby, forcing families into further economic hardship. As a result, children may join armed forces or groups to secure daily food and survival. Conflict is also likely to disrupt children's education. This study examines the use of children as soldiers in armed conflict and the impact it has on economic development in African countries. The result shows that, both child recruitment and child labor can potentially lead a country to extreme poverty and may often deny children from basic school education. [Author Abstract]

40.)   **Park, A.**

Diamonds in the RUF: Mercy, reintegration and the crafting of childhood. The case of child soldiers in Sierra Leone.
Ph.D. dissertation, York University (Canada). 2006.

Child soldiers were principal perpetrators of egregious atrocities during Sierra Leone's decade-long civil war. Yet, in the post-conflict period, instead of facing criminal trial, children are absorbed into non-governmental organisations (NGOs) that have tasked themselves with the work of building a peaceable nation through reintegrated child combatants. The absolution of child soldiers of their criminality in Sierra Leone's war crimes tribunal, the Special Court, can be understood as an exercise of mercy, which expels child perpetrators outside of law's violence. 'Hegemonic childhood', which defines children as evolving, innocent, amoral and politically incompetent, forms the basis for children's merciful exculpation. Despite its emergence in the modern, capitalist west, hegemonic childhood is increasingly globalised, and institutions like international law play a central role in the neo-colonial expansion of the hegemonic ideal in the service of forging a global moral community. 'The child' of children's rights discourse, moreover, is promulgated in NGOs. The NGO on which I base my research, Connecting for Peace, works towards crafting and subjectivating hegemonic childhood in the reintegration of child soldiers. While the suffering child as metonym for global Southern pathology invites the intervention of the international community and its (neo-colonising) rescue efforts, children in Sierra Leone also use hegemonic discourse in order to make demands. While efforts of international law, the Special Court and Connecting for Peace craft a particular version of childhood, Sierra Leone's Truth and Reconciliation Commission suggests ways to re-vision childhood in order more meaningfully to involve children's participation. [Author Abstract]

41.)   **Reed, C. V.**

The reintegration of female child soldiers into society: Fact and fiction.

M.P.P. thesis, Georgetown University. 2010.

The use of child soldiers is one of the most universally condemned human rights abuses in the world, yet an estimated 300,000 children are currently believed to be fighting in over 30 conflicts around the globe. Due to their relative naiveté and malleability, children are forced to play numerous roles as child soldiers; including that of porters, cooks, fighters on the front line and sex slaves. While many of these children die before they are released others escape, are rescued or are returned by their captors. These children then face the daunting task of reintegrating into society. Despite the broad nature of the issue, and its huge individual and societal impacts, relatively little is known about child soldiers, their time in service and their experience of reintegration. What little research is available focuses almost exclusively on male child soldiers. Despite this, female child soldiers make up an estimate 30% of all child soldiers and, due to their gender specific experiences, often face greater challenges in reintegration. Drawing from a data set from northern Uganda, this paper explores the roles of female child soldiers in the Lord's Resistance Army (LRA), and how their experiences while with the LRA and upon return to society affect their reintegration experience. Ultimately, this paper finds that specific war-time experiences greatly affect reintegration and that the provision of appropriate programs and support upon return can positively impact a girl's reintegration experience. [Author Abstract]

42.)   **Reta, R.**

Negotiating the Release of Child Soldiers in War: Engaging Non-state Armed Groups during Periods of Conflict.

M.A. thesis, McGill University (Canada). 2009.

The persistent use of child soldiers in war continues to be a serious problem for many countries locked in conflicts around the world, yet surprisingly little attention has been given to those actors who are recruiting children in the greatest numbers: namely, non-state armed groups (NSAs). In recent years, several NSAs have entered into formal commitments with UNICEF to end their child recruitment practices; what is more interesting, they have done so during periods of active conflict. Why have these armed groups signed such agreements? Are there observable patterns among these NSAs that could better help us predict the likelihood of engaging with other groups in the future? This Masters thesis endeavours to look more closely at the nature of these specific actors employing children in war, and the dynamics surrounding negotiated agreements, in order to answer the question: why do non-state armed groups agree to end their child recruitment practices during periods of ongoing conflict? [Author Abstract]

43.)   **Ryan, C. E.**

Raised by war: child soldiers of Southern Sudan during the Second Civil War.

Ph.D. dissertation, University of London, School of Oriental and African Studies (United Kingdom). 2009.

Child soldiers are addressed in literature and by non-governmental organisations as being victims of warfare, while the question of their level of personal and political agency goes unexamined. This thesis aims to address and correct this oversimplification of their role. In order to unravel the complexity and reveal the vast experiences of child soldiers, the empirical research includes over one hundred interviews with former child soldiers from the Southern Sudanese Second Civil War, non-governmental agency workers and civil society members in Southern Sudan. The testimonies of the child soldiers create a rich picture by providing them a voice through which their stories are told using their own words. Against this backdrop, testimonies from non-governmental agency workers and civil society members serve to highlight the gulf of understanding between theory and practice, drawing out dissimilarities in opinion as they interpret the experiences and capabilities of the child soldiers whose interests they supposedly represent. Together, these perspectives serve as a critique of the existing body of literature and suggest further areas of research. This thesis expands consideration of the child solider role beyond one of the `victim's by adopting an empirically based analysis of their political awareness, struggles and agency. Through this I demonstrate the importance of making their personal motivations and subsequent reflections an integral part of the way in which the subject of child soldiers is studied. The value and insight revealed in this analysis opens the door both to future research regarding children in conflict and to a shift in the approach of civil society engagement in the field. [Author Abstract]

44.)   **Samphansakul, A.**

Child soldiers and intrastate armed conflicts: An analysis of the recruitments of child soldiers in civil wars between 2001 and 2003.

M.A. thesis, University of North Texas. 2008.

This thesis examines why some governments and rebel organizations but not others recruit children to be child soldiers. The theory posits that if a country fights in a civil war of long duration, armed groups are more likely to recruit children as soldiers. I find that the probability of child soldier recruitment increases when a country experiences following conditions: a longer duration of civil war, a large proportion of battle deaths, a large number of refugees, a high infant mortality rate, and the presence of alluvial diamonds. An increase in education expenditures and civil liberties would decrease the probability of child soldier recruitments. [Author Abstract]

45.) **Shepler, S. A.**

Conflicted childhoods: Fighting over child soldiers in Sierra Leone.

Ph.D. dissertation, University of California, Berkeley. 2005.

This dissertation examines how Sierra Leoneans make strategic use of the flood of international resources--both material and discursive--that have been directed to the problem of reintegration of child soldiers starting in the mid-1990s. The work is based on eighteen months of ethnographic fieldwork in Sierra Leone in Interim Care Centers for former child soldiers, in schools struggling to integrate children whose education has been disrupted by war, in non-formal apprenticeship programs, and in selected communities where former child soldiers have been reunified with their families. The decade-long civil war in Sierra Leone was complex, with different meanings for participants depending on class, ethnic group, gender, and geographical location. This work traces the variable experiences of the war in five distinct field sites within Sierra Leone, each with its own trajectory and timeline. It contrasts the Sierra Leonean model of childhood--described with reference to four key practices: child labor, fosterage, apprenticeship education, and secret society initiation--with the Western model of childhood that underpins the NGO practices designed to help former child soldiers reintegrate into society. "Child Soldier" as a category is co-created by Sierra Leoneans and Westerners in social practice. By adopting the Western identity of innocent youth, children in Sierra Leone are moving from a blunt kind of power, to a power legitimated through international structures. The techniques behind the creation of "child soldier" as a post-war identity have unexpected political effects. Struggles over childhood and child rights in post war Sierra Leone are productive sites in that they become the locus for all kinds of other political struggles. In particular, the work compares the experiences of formal and informal reintegrators, boy soldiers and girl soldiers, and children affiliated with the (RUF) rebels and the (CDF) local militias. This dissertation shows that in some ways Western interventions designed to ease the reintegration of former child soldiers in fact make that reintegration more difficult. The practical conclusion is that programs for former child soldiers should work within local understandings of child protection, for example through child fosterage and apprenticeship, rather than through excessive institutionalization and reliance on Western models. [Author Abstract]

46.)   **Souris, R. N.**

Does defective moral development ever excuse?
The case of adult soldiers recruited as children.
Ph.D. dissertation, American University. 2014.

This dissertation proposes to introduce a new excuse into international criminal law for persons who lack normal moral perception in accordance with international standards and who have impaired practical reasoning, if they developed these defect through no fault of their own. The main ground for the excuse is that by lacking normal moral perception in accordance with international standards, these persons are deprived of the fair opportunity to choose to obey the law. I identify adult soldiers who were recruited at a young age into extreme armed groups and for whom it is reasonable to expect would develop emotional disturbances in response to their experiences as child soldiers in those groups, and who, did in fact develop such disturbances, which distorts their adult moral judgment and impairs their practical reasoning. [Author Abstract]

47.)   **Stout, K.**

"Silences and Empty Spaces" -- The Reintegration of Girl Child Soldiers in Uganda: Gendering the Problem and Engendering Solutions.

M.S. thesis, University of Toronto (Canada). 2013.

This thesis examines the experiences of girl child soldiers in Uganda in order to explore the gender gaps that exist in post-conflict programming and to engender meaningful policy solutions that target these gaps. This thesis uses a gender lens to analyze the challenges faced by Ugandan girls and to explore how entrenched gender norms feed into a singular narrative of conflict - dangerous boys and traumatized girls - that renders particular combatants - and their unique needs - invisible. Adopting a feminist methodology that prioritizes the importance of girls' narratives and self-perceptions, the author argues that girl child soldiers must be meaningfully included in the design and implementation of programming aimed at serving their needs. A participatory action research methodology is presented as a promising way forward. It can help address specific gendered challenges in the post-conflict environment, while also recognizing and drawing upon the resiliency and strengths of the girl child soldiers themselves. [Author Abstract]

48.) **Stuebing, D. L.**

Return to childhood: An analysis of the reintegration of child soldiers.

M.A. thesis, Saint Mary's University (Canada). 2005.

Beginning with a child-rights framework guided by recommendations in the Machel report and programmatic 'best-practices' in rehabilitation "Return to Childhood" analyses the reintegration of child soldiers in three case studies, Mozambique, Uganda and Sierra Leone. Case studies were chosen for reasons including documentation availability, regional and colonial diversity within sub-Saharan Africa and difference in conflict status. The research was based on qualitative comparative analysis of policies and programming for child soldiers. Case-study governments are parties to the Convention on the Rights of the Child and other international legislation. With varying degrees of recognition for their obligation as duty-bearers, these governments created or allowed an environment that supported programming for demobilized child soldiers. The findings of this research indicate that programming which included psycho-social rehabilitation, family reunification, education and skills training resulted in varying degrees of reintegration hampered by continued instability and lack of systemic support by governments. [Author Abstract]

49.)   **Tynes, R. M.**

Child Soldiers, Armed Conflicts, and Tactical Innovations.

Ph.D. dissertation, State University of New York at Albany. 2011.

Most armed conflicts in the late 20th and early 21st century involve the use of child soldiers. Children have been used in wars before the modern era, but this study argues that a shift has occurred in contemporary conflicts. Child soldier use has become a tactical innovation. Fighting factions utilize children as soldiers in order to gain an advantage on the battlefield. Several different analytical approaches are used in order to test the argument. First, a large-N regression analysis (1987-2007) reveals that depending on the dyadic relationship between government and opposition forces, intensity of war, military expenditures per GDP, political terror, troop size, polity and education correlate with child soldier use. Second, a historical analysis suggests that a century of youth empowerment, an increase in the ambiguity regarding the sanctity of civilian life in war, and exponential leaps in war technology all contributed to a shift in norms about children in the battlefield. Third, a social network analysis demonstrates the structural connection between groups that use child soldiers. The tactical innovation flows along pathways linked by multiple guerilla learning centers. The most prominent center is the Libyan guerilla training camps of the 1980s. Lastly, a single case study of the civil war in Sierra Leone offers insight into the ground-level dynamics of child solider use and how the practice can produce political opportunities. Policy suggestions centered on prevention, compellence and protection are offered in the concluding section. [Author Abstract]

50.)   **Ward, M. A.**

Child soldiers and noncompliance of international human rights law.

M.A. thesis, California State University, Fullerton. 2004.

This thesis examines the reasons why children continue to be used as child soldiers in developing countries even though their government is party to international law that prohibits this use. Human rights advocates maintain that states can "get away" with noncompliance because of weak monitoring mechanisms and that these states only ratify relevant treaties to enhance their international reputation. It is argued that many factors, other than only wanting to enhance reputations of states, exist to explain the lack of compliance of developing countries to the Optional Protocol to the Convention on the Rights of the Child on the Involvement of Children in Armed Conflict. Lack of funding and resources, temporal dimensions, vagueness of treaty wording, weak monitoring mechanisms, and the "Westernization" of human rights all contribute to problems of enforcement. Weak governments, divided states, and the involvement in conflicts contribute significantly to this noncompliance. [Author Abstract]

51.) **Waschefort, C. A.**

Child soldiers and international law: progressing towards an era of application?

Ph.D. dissertation, University of London, School of Oriental and African Studies (United Kingdom). 2012.

Academic legal literature has focused heavily on the creation and content of norms prohibiting the use and recruitment of child soldiers, rather than on how to apply these norms more effectively. In this thesis, I argue that this focus must now be redirected towards a greater emphasis on application. Effective application does not require major changes to any entity or functionary engaged in child soldier prevention; rather, it requires the constant reassessment and refinement of all such entities and functionaries, and here, some changes are required. International judicial, quasi-judicial and non-judicial entities and functionaries most relevant to child soldier prevention are critically assessed.

Specific areas where these entities and functionaries can be improved in their effective application of child soldier prohibitive norms are identified, and the implementation of the suggested changes are analysed. However, prior to analysing the application of the relevant norms, I analyse the enforceability of these norms, to determine whether they can indeed be applied. In this regard, I find that although there are shortcomings in these norms, they are nonetheless enforceable. I further argue that the nature of the legal regime to which a specific norm belongs, impacts on the enforceability of the relevant norm. This is due to the nature of the obligations created, as well as the enforcement mechanisms that belong to the relevant legal regime's, in this case, international human rights law, international humanitarian law and international criminal law. The conclusions of this study are based, in part, on interviews conducted with individuals engaged with child soldier prevention at the highest level. The Democratic Republic of the Congo (DRC) is used as a case study against which the study's conclusions are tested; based on field research in the DRC. [Author Abstract]

52.)   **Whitmire, L.**

The creation and evolution of the Acholi ethnic identity.

M.A. thesis, Clemson University. 2013.

On March 5th, 2012, the Kony 2012 video was released by the authors and director of Invisible Children , and Uganda instantaneously became the center of young America's focus. This graphic video contained disturbing images of child soldiers and dead children, aiming to draw sympathy and awareness to the ongoing problem the Lord's Resistance Army's violent attacks on the Acholi of Northern Uganda and recruitment measures. While many Americans responded to the video's urgent request for support by encouraging the government to act, others adhered to the popular belief that this conflict was nothing more than another tribal conflict among a backwards group of people. In my African history class that same week, students voiced their concern over the violent images they saw, but unconsciously, they also displayed an ignorance of the origins of such conflicts in Africa. To someone with very little knowledge of Africa's history, this situation would seemingly offer an obvious solution such as the one the Kony 2012 video presented to its viewers: kill Joseph Kony and the situation will resolve itself. To Africanist, particularly those who study Uganda's history, this conflict reflects issues that extend beyond the current conflict. In order to understand the origins of this conflict, people need a better understanding of the largest ethnic group affected by it, the Acholi of northern Uganda. This thesis provides a history of the Acholi that clarifies their role in Ugandan politics. The larger purpose of this thesis is to illustrate the factors that contributed to the creation and evolution of the Acholi ethnic identity and how their ethnic identity influenced their relationships with those outside of their ethnic group. The Acholi identity continuously evolved because of their interaction with other groups, as well as their inclusion into a larger socio-political institution. Through processes of negotiation, the Acholi the pre-colonial period adjusted to the changes the colonial and post-colonial periods instigated. While this thesis does not cover the present day conflict, the role the Acholi have in it becomes more evident through this study. [Author Abstract]

53.)   **Wu, F.**

Protection of Children in Armed Conflict.

LL.M. thesis, Renmin University of China (People's Republic of China). 2008.

International law attempts to afford civilians special protection from the effects and inhumanity of armed conflict. While, the forms of violence today have given rise to an increase in the numbers of civilian victims, and particularly of children, who, an account of their special vulnerability, are the most seriously affected. The active participation of children in hostilities, too, is a disturbing factor serious enough to justify the increasing attention the subject is receiving within the international community. Current statistics, however, portray a sobering and distinctive trend in modern warfare: the deliberate victimization of children and the blatant disregard for their human rights. Despite the United Nation's (UN) remarkable achievements with peace-keeping missions, ethnic conflicts continue to arise and new states continue to expand the international community. At least three hundred thousand children, some as young as eight years old, currently serve in armed conflicts around the world. This Note focuses on international attempts to protect children in armed conflict and reduce the use of child soldiers. The global community must work collectively to update existing international laws to reflect the increased participation of children in hostilities and to initiate the necessary enforcement and rehabilitative mechanisms. International Humanitarian Law governs the conduct of armed conflict and impose restrictions based on moral, legal, philosophical, religious and political considerations. Current international humanitarian law, as defined in the four Geneva Conventions of 1949, the two additional Protocols of 1977 attempts to insulate children from the tragedies of war. The injuries children receive as a result of modern warfare, however, affront the underlying humanitarian ideals that motivated the creation of these laws. Moreover, the continued use of child combatants illustrates the international community's failure to protect the world's children. To place this issue in perspective, the writer then illustrates the current condition of child soldier in different counties especially in Iraq and Africa. Deliberate targeting of children in modern warfare and the increased use of children in armed conflict badly hurt children and violate their human right. The most serious aberration from international humanitarian ideals, however, stems from the recruitment and utilization of young boys and girls as child soldiers. International human rights law embodied in the CRC currently sets the minimum age for recruitment and participation in armed conflict at fifteen years of age; however, children as young as seven continue to serve in armies across the world. Besides the forced recruitment, a vast number of children voluntarily join the military regimes. Often the culture of violence, the desperation for food, the need for security or the drive to avenge the deaths of family members prompts such unforced recruitment. The motivation of children to arm themselves includes war, poverty, education and family ect. Without addressing the roots of the conflict, children will continue to volunteer; therefore, even if the international community establishes an effective ban on forced recruitment, it alone will not suffice. Effects of Warfare on Children are wild and serious. Malnutrition, disease, sexual exploitation and physical injury constitute only a few of the tangible wounds deliberately inflicted on children. The suffer of psychological trauma as a result of armed conflict becomes an incurable hurt on their innocent heart. International Criminal Court (ICC) as we know was constructed to prosecute those accused of war crimes and crimes against humanity. The July 1998 Rome Statute of the ICC established the recruitment and use of child soldiers under the age of fifteen as a war crime. Together, these two movements have the potential to provide better protection for the world's youth and a means to enforce and to punish those who violate human rights treaties. Besides the ICC, the next Part enlists documents of international laws that focus on children. In 1924, the League of Nations unanimously adopted the Declaration of the Rights of the Child, thereby adopting the first global charter focusing on children's rights. In 1948, the UN General Assembly proclaimed the equal and inalienable rights of all human beings, regardless of age, by adopting the Universal Declaration of Human Rights (UDHR). The first UN instrument devoted solely to children's rights is the Declaration of the Rights of the Child in 1959 which sets forth the best interests of the child standard and demands that those responsible for education and advisement utilize this standard as a guiding principle. Entering into force in 1990, the Convention on the Rights of the Child (CRC) served as a milestone in the establishment and recognition of children's rights. While as the sole super power in the world, the United States does not support the CRC and will not endorse global efforts to protect children from the atrocities of armed conflict. Its attitude of opposition to efforts promoting a global agreement to ban the use of soldiers under the age of eighteen badly hindered the international effort of protecting children in armed conflict. Therefore, the U.S. Congress finally adopted a Congressional Resolution condemning the use of child soldiers in the Defense Appropriations Authorization Act for 1999. Even the Resolution does not bind the United States, it constitutes a significant step in the right direction. To stop the use of children as soldiers and improve their statue, the writer puts forward some suggestions as follow: Ratify the Optional Protocol on Involvement of Children in Armed Conflict and other legal instruments relevant to the protection of children in armed conflict. Ensure that national laws are compatible with international legal standards. Promote systematic demobilization of child soldiers in all countries. Build capacities for appropriate psycho-social support and response to ex-child combatants. Develop prevention strategies to reduce the factors that make children vulnerable to "voluntary" recruitment. The International

Committee of the Red Cross legitimately labeled the twentieth century, the "century of war." In the past century, the line between civilians and combatants blurred, military groups deliberately targeted and recruited children and entire generations have grown up amidst armed conflict. Concurrently, the twentieth century produced universal humanitarian treaties that imposed limits on warfare, afforded children special protection and specifically recognized the inherent rights of the child. Unfortunately, problems remain in the effectiveness and enforceability of these rules of law and as a result, children remain vulnerable to the tragic effects of armed conflict. The international community must implement stronger standards that reflect the global awareness and sensitivity toward the plight of the world's children. The international community must work together to monitor human rights violations, to demobilize child soldiers and to prosecute offenders. To create a more humane world and to further improve the status of children, the international community must use its collective authority to ensure that states observe the standards aimed at protecting the world's children. [Author Abstract]

Locating Dissertations and Theses

A. Purchase

Many of the dissertations and theses listed in this bibliography are available for purchase through UMI Dissertation Express:

http://disexpress.umi.com/dxweb

By Fax:

800-864-0019

By Mail:

789 E. Eisenhower Parkway, P.O. Box 1346, Ann Arbor, Michigan 48106-1346

800-521-3042

B. Interlibrary Loan

Dissertations and theses may also be requested through Interlibrary Loan via your local public, college or university library.